About the Book

Jimmy Carter was little known a year before the Presidential election of 1976. He came from a small town in Georgia. No one from the Deep South had been elected President since 1848. He was the past Governor of a Southern state. Few had even heard of him outside Georgia. How could he be elected President?

But Jimmy Carter was determined. He traveled around the country meeting people everywhere. He spoke sincerely about the country's problems. He said the government didn't care about the people's needs. Everywhere people listened.

And on January 20, 1977, Jimmy Carter, the little-known man from Georgia, became the 39th President of the United States.

Jimmy Carter

by Charles Mercer
illustrations by Ruth Sanderson

A See and Read Biography

G. P. Putnam's Sons   New York

Text copyright © 1977 by Charles Mercer
Illustrations copyright © 1977 by Ruth Sanderson
All rights reserved. Published simultaneously in
Canada by Longman Canada Limited, Toronto.
PRINTED IN THE UNITED STATES OF AMERICA
Library of Congress Cataloging in Publication Data
Mercer, Charles E Jimmy Carter
1. Carter, Jimmy, 1924-   —Juvenile literature.
2. Presidents—United States—Biography—Juvenile
literature. (1. Carter, Jimmy, 1924-   2. Presidents)
I. Sanderson, Ruth. II. Title. E873.M47 1977
973.926′092′4   [92]   77-1861
ISBN 0-399-61094-4 lib. bdg.

Third Impression

Jimmy Carter

Jimmy Carter grew up on a farm near Plains, Georgia. His father grew peanuts. When Jimmy was six years old, he decided to go into the peanut business himself.

Peanuts grow underground, on

the roots of vines. There are about fifty nuts to a vine. Jimmy pulled up the vines, loaded his wagon with nuts, and took them home. There he soaked the nuts overnight and boiled them in salt water.

Next Jimmy put about a half pound of boiled peanuts in each of twenty bags. He filled a basket with the bags and carried them two miles down the railroad tracks to Plains. Nearly every Saturday, he sold his peanuts for a nickel a bag, and he didn't go home until he had sold every one.

To this day, Jimmy Carter says that boiled fresh peanuts taste much better than the roasted kind you buy in stores.

Jimmy was born James Earl Carter, Jr., on October 1, 1924. His father was a successful farmer and businessman. His mother, Lillian, was a nurse.

Both of his parents' families had lived in Georgia for generations. Jimmy, his younger brother, Billy, and his sisters, Gloria and Ruth, were the fifth generation of the Carter family to live on the same land.

When Jimmy was growing up on the farm, most of his friends were black. They worked as well as played together. They plowed the fields, using mules; they cut wood, stacked peanut vines, fed chickens, mended fences.

In later years, Jimmy remembered, "We ran, swam, rode horses, drove wagons and floated on rafts together. We misbehaved together and shared the same punishments. We built and lived in the same tree houses and played cards and ate at the same table. But we never went to the same church or school."

In those days in Georgia, and in
some other states, *segregation* was
the law. That meant that blacks
and whites were separated from

one another when they went to
school or church, when they rode
on buses or trains, even when
they went to public rest rooms.

Jimmy's father believed in segregation. Jimmy's mother did not. Lillian Carter believed it was wrong to separate people because of the color of their skin.

A man called William Johnson lived near the Carter farm. He was the bishop of the African Methodist Episcopal Church in a half dozen states. He was an important man. He was a good friend of Mr. Carter's. Still, Mr. Carter never invited the bishop into his home. Bishop Johnson was black.

When the bishop wanted to talk to Mr. Carter, his chauffeur drove

him to the Carter farm. The chauffeur announced the bishop at the
back door. Mr. Carter would come
out and talk to Bishop Johnson in
the back yard.

It was different for the bishop's son Alvan. He went to school in Boston, where there was no segregation at that time. And he was a

friend of Lillian Carter's. When Alvan Johnson came home on vacation, he was welcomed at the front door by Mrs. Carter. She would invite him into the living room to visit. Mr. Carter would slip out the back door. He was "trying to pretend it wasn't happening," Jimmy later said. But Jimmy's mother kept on doing what she felt was right.

The Carters had one of the first radios in the Plains area. One day the blacks who worked on the farm asked Mr. Carter if they could listen to the world heavyweight boxing championship on the radio.

The fight was between the black boxer and world champion Joe Louis and the white German champion Max Schmeling. Some people felt that a victory for Schmeling would prove that whites were stronger than blacks. Mr. Carter wanted Schmeling to win, and he was sure he would.

On the night of the fight, Mr. Carter, Jimmy, a few white friends and dozens of blacks gathered under a large mulberry tree in the yard. They put the radio on a windowsill of the house and turned it up loud. Then they listened to the announcer as he described Joe Louis' knocking out Max Schmeling in the first round.

The blacks in the Carter yard were quiet. They thanked Mr. Carter and left. They walked a good distance from the yard. Then.they began to yell with delight over the victory of their hero. Jimmy Carter never forgot the happy shouts of his black friends that night.

Jimmy was closer to his mother than to his father. He could talk to "Mama" about anything. She was the first to make him realize that old ideas, such as the one that white people were better or stronger than black people, were not necessarily good ideas.

Until Jimmy was fourteen years old, Mr. Carter insisted on cutting his son's hair. And he used mule shears. Once when Jimmy was going away to visit his grandparents, his father decided to give him a haircut. But Mr. Carter's hand slipped and the mule shears took off a big chunk. To try to make the hair even in length, Mr. Carter kept cutting—until he had cut off all of Jimmy's hair!

When Jimmy came home, his grandmother wrote a note to his mother. "He's a fine boy, but he acts real peculiar. He's the only child I've ever seen who eats and sleeps with his cap on!"

Jimmy and his brother and sisters all had nicknames for each other. Billy was "Buck," Gloria was "Gogo," and Ruth was "Boopy Doop." They called Jimmy "Hot." As Gloria recalled, "when Jimmy was a boy, we called him 'Hot'—he was always fired up—but he never liked it. He was always up to something."

When Jimmy took on something, he gave it his full effort. He was an ambitious boy. To him, ambition meant that you must work hard to get what you want; you must take risks; you must never be afraid to try nor fear to lose all in your trying.

This is exactly the way Jimmy ran his peanut business—from the time he was six years old, walking the tracks into Plains.

The years when Jimmy was growing up were called the Great Depression. Millions of people were out of work. Millions were hungry. A grown man working on the farms around Plains earned a dollar a day. Women were paid 75¢ and children 25¢ for a day's work in the fields. So Jimmy, like everyone else, saw it was wise to use his brains and do his best to make money.

Jimmy worked long hours at his boiled-peanut business. He

would earn as much as $5 a day! He could have put the money in a bank, where it would have collected a small interest. Instead he decided to take a chance. He asked his father to buy cotton with his earnings. In those Depression years cotton was selling for the low price of $25 a bale. By the time Jimmy was nine he had bought five bales of cotton. He kept the cotton in one of his father's storehouses. When Jimmy was thirteen the price of cotton reached $90 a bale. He sold his cotton for $450. It had cost him $125. At that time $450 was enough money to buy five small houses in Plains. The rent from these houses brought the industrious Jimmy $16.50 a month.

No wonder Jimmy Carter later became known as one of the smartest businessmen in Georgia.

Jimmy was a good student who got high grades in school. He liked sports, but he wasn't big enough to play on the football team. He loved tennis and played a good game.

After high school, Jimmy wanted to go to the U.S. Naval Academy in Annapolis, Maryland. But Jimmy was afraid he couldn't get in. He had flat feet. He stood on Coke bottles and rolled back and forth hoping to raise his arches! But with the help of his father Jimmy got in anyway. And he did well at the academy.

The summer before graduation, Jimmy came home on leave. One afternoon he was driving around town when he saw his sister Ruth in the Baptist Church yard with a friend. He had met Rosalynn Smith before, but he had never paid any attention to her. Now he

stopped the car and invited this
lovely, dark-haired girl to the mov-
ies that evening.

The next morning, Jimmy's
mother asked him how he liked
Rosalynn. Jimmy answered with-
out any hesitation. "Mama, she's
the girl I want to marry."

But when Jimmy asked Rosalynn to marry him, she said no. She was still young, and she wanted to be sure he knew what he was asking. Later, when he proposed again, she said yes. They were married soon after his graduation from the Naval Academy, in 1946.

Rosalynn and Jimmy had a lot in common. Her family had lived in the Plains area as long as his. They were both members of the Plains Baptist Church. They were both intelligent. But most important was the fact that Rosalynn was as ambitious and hardworking as Jimmy. They shared the same goals.

Rosalynn and Jimmy looked forward to their life in the Navy. Jimmy wanted to join the Navy's nuclear-submarine program. The head of the program was Admiral Hyman Rickover, a brilliant, tough officer. During the interview Admiral Rickover looked Jimmy straight in the eye and never smiled.

"How did you stand in your class at the Naval Academy?" he asked.

"Sir," Jimmy replied, "I stood fifty-ninth in a class of eight hundred twenty."

He sat back, waiting for the admiral's compliment on his high

class standing. Instead the admiral asked, "Did you do your best?"

Jimmy started to say yes, but then he answered truthfully, "No, sir, I didn't *always* do my best."

Rickover looked at Jimmy Carter for a long time; then he asked, "Why not?"

Shaken, Jimmy turned and left the room slowly.

"Admiral Rickover," Jimmy recalls, "had a profound effect on my life—perhaps more than anyone except my parents. He was unbelievably hardworking and competent, and he demanded total dedication from his subordinates."

In later years Jimmy Carter would write his life story and call it *Why Not the Best?*

In 1953 Jimmy's father died of cancer. Jimmy went home to be with him. Jimmy did not always agree with his father, but he loved him. During those last days,

Jimmy and his father had good talks together. Besides his wife and Jimmy, there was one other person Mr. Carter most enjoyed talking to during that time. He was a black friend.

After his father died, Jimmy decided to quit the Navy. He would go home to Plains to run the family business. Rosalynn thought Jimmy was wrong to give up a promising career under Admiral Rickover. Rosalynn did not want to go back to small-town life in Plains where, with only 450 people, everyone seemed to know what everyone else was doing.

She and Jimmy had the biggest argument they had ever had over moving back to Plains. But in the end Rosalynn went home with Jimmy.

It was hard going for the young Carters. Jimmy grew peanuts and sold fertilizer to farmers. In his first year he made less than $200. Rosalynn worked full-time with him. Gradually the business grew. Jimmy stopped growing peanuts. Instead he bought and sold to other farmers. He stored their peanuts in his warehouses. Today it is a big, prosperous business managed by his brother Billy.

Jimmy got involved with his town. He became a deacon in the Plains Baptist Church. He served on the school board and was the local scoutmaster.

In 1962 Jimmy wanted to run for state senator in Georgia. Jimmy was a Democrat. In the South the Democratic party was the strongest and most popular party. Whoever was chosen to run as the Democratic candidate was almost sure to win.

A primary election was held to pick the candidate. Jimmy lost the election by just a few votes. He was sure more people had voted for him. He was convinced there had been cheating in the counting of the votes. He went to court, won his case, and was declared the winner of the Democratic primary election. He went on to become a state senator.

Four years later he ran for governor of Georgia . . . and lost. But Jimmy would not give up. He was determined. He spent the next four years giving speeches and getting the voters to know him. In 1970 he ran again and won.

During the 1960s there was a strong effort in Georgia and the rest of the South to *desegregate*.

46

Desegregation means to break
down the laws and the feelings
about separating people because
of the color of their skin. Some
Southerners no longer wanted
black people to be treated differ-
ently from white people. They
wanted them to go to the same
schools and churches and to have
the same opportunities.

Many Southern whites did not want changes. But Jimmy Carter was among those who did. He knew that change must come. But he also knew he could not last as a politician in Georgia if he worked for quick change. Too many people were against it. So he was cautious. This made enemies. People were not sure what he really believed. Some whites said he was really for desegregation. Some blacks said he was really against desegregation. But many blacks had faith that Jimmy Carter was their friend.

Most people agree he was a good governor of Georgia from 1970 to 1974. He made state government work better. He got people to cool their anger. By law he could not run for another term as governor. So he, Rosalynn, and their little daughter Amy went home to Plains. Their three sons were grown up, with families of their own.

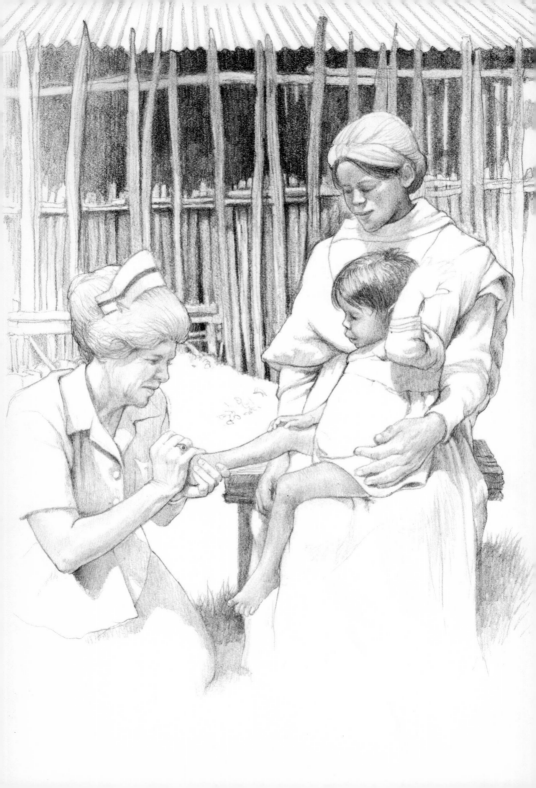

Jimmy remained close to his mother. He admired the spirit of "Miss Lillian," as she was known around Plains. When she was almost seventy years old, she had joined the Peace Corps and gone off to India for two years as a nurse.

One day after returning to Plains, Jimmy went to see his mother. Miss Lillian was not feeling well that day. She was lying in one of the twin beds in her

room. Jimmy sat down on the other bed and put his feet on his mother's bed. Then he said, "Mama, I've decided to run for president of the United States."

Miss Lillian looked at her son for a long time. Then she said, "Jimmy, take your feet off my bed."

If she had not known he was bright and steady, she might have thought him crazy. No one from the Deep South had been elected president since 1848. Jimmy lived in a little country town few people had ever heard of. He was the past governor of a Southern state,

and who had heard of him outside of Georgia? He was a slight, shy man. He had a low voice and a ready smile. How could he be elected president?

When Miss Lillian told Jimmy to take his feet off her bed, it was her way of saying, "Your idea of becoming president is so crazy I'll pretend you never said it."

But she knew what a determined person Jimmy was. He took a job with the Democratic National Committee. He traveled around the country meeting politicians and campaign workers. "Hello, I'm Jimmy Carter . . ." he said everywhere.

Jimmy flew nearly half a million miles about the country. He gave 1,500 speeches. He gathered a small staff of helpers. Rosalynn was among them. These helpers were not the oldtime Democratic politicians. They were young and old, but they wanted the same thing. They wanted change in the government.

Jimmy said too many people were out of work. He said that the government in Washington did not care enough about the needs of ordinary people.

Jimmy inspired confidence. He promised to make things better.

And he promised to keep his promises. At the Democratic National Convention in New York, in July, 1976, Jimmy Carter was nominated as his party's candidate for president. He would run against President Gerald Ford, a Republican.

How could he beat a President who was already in office and well known? Did enough people know who Jimmy Carter was and what he thought? Had people stopped saying "Jimmy who?"

213552

It would be a close race on Election Day, November 2, 1976. As the votes came in late that night, a pattern took shape. Ford was strong among well-off people who did not want change. They feared expensive government programs and higher taxes. Carter was very strong in the South, where people wanted a Southerner to become president. He was strong with blacks everywhere and with Puerto Ricans and Chicanos. All of them were the voters who had suffered the most from high prices and the lack of jobs. Carter won about 51 percent of the popular vote. Ford won about 48 percent.

60

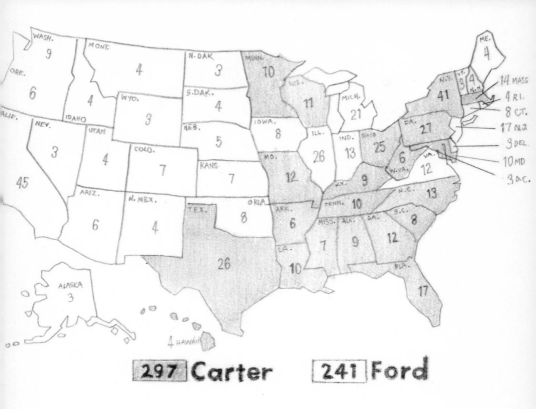

297 Carter **241 Ford**

It was a close race, but Jimmy Carter had realized his ambition. He had convinced enough Americans that he was the best man for the job. On January 20, 1977, he took the oath of office as the thirty-ninth president of the United States.

Friends and family members who attended the inauguration in Washington still remember Jimmy Carter's words the morning after Election Day: "I see the sun rising on a new day, a beautiful spirit in the country . . . a commitment to the future."

About the Author

Charles Mercer is the author of more than twenty novels and works of non-fiction besides scores of stories and articles in national magazines. At one time he covered political events for the Washington *Post*. He and his wife now live in New York, where he is an editor of books for young people.

About the Artist

Ruth Sanderson was born and brought up in Massachusetts. She was educated at Denison University and Paier School of Art, from which she was graduated.

When she is not involved in her art, she spends her time raising and training a quarter horse, riding being one of her great loves.

Ms. Sanderson also illustrated *Grandma's Beach Surprise* and the See and Read Biography, *Walt Disney*.

DATE DUE